URSA

SPACE REVEALED

SPACE EXPLORATION

by
Claudia Martin

BEARPORT
PUBLISHING

Minneapolis, Minnesota

Credits

Cover and title page, © NASA/NASA Image and Video Library and © mode_list/Adobe Stock; 4, © Bruno Mader/Adobe Stock; 5, © NASA/NASA Image and Video Library; 6M, © Mark Garlick/Science Photo Library; 6B, © GL Archive/Alamy Stock; 7, © John A. Davis/Shutterstock; 8L, © Sheila Terry/Science Photo Library; 8R, © New York Public Library/Science Photo Library; 9TL, © nicku/Shutterstock; 9TR, © Joseph Brown/Joseph Brown; 9BL, © Michael W. Gorth/Michael W. Gorth; 9BR, © ESA/NASA; 10, © QA International/Science Source/Science Photo Library; 11T, © shooarts/Shutterstock; 11BL, © Aliona Ursu/Shutterstock; 11BR, © Andy Vinnikov/Shutterstock; 12T, © Tim Brown/Science Photo Library; 12B, © Myrabella/Myrabella; 13TL, © JPL/NASA; 13TR, © ESO/ESO; 13M, © Rosetta/NAVCAM/ESA; 13B, © MarcelClemens/Shutterstock; 14–15, © oxameel/Shutterstock; 16T, © lisheng2121/Shutterstock; 16B, © SPL/Shutterstock; 17T, © lisheng2121/Shutterstock; 17M, © Carlos Clarivan/Science Photo Library; 17B, © underworld/Shutterstock; 18T, © coolvectormaker/Adobe Stock; 18B, © Marshall Space Flight Center/NASA; 19, © Marshall Space Flight Center/NASA; 20T, © Goddard/Chris Gunn/NASA; 20B, © Goddard/Chris Gunn/NASA; 21, © GSFC/NASA; 22T, © 3d-man/Shutterstock; 22B, © NRAO/AUI/NASA; 23, © imagechina/Alamy Stock; 24T, © Sergii Syzonenko/Shutterstock; 24M, © NASA/NASA; 24B, © NASA/NASA; 25, © Artsiom Petrushenka/NASA/Shutterstock; 26T, © NASA/NASA; 26B, © JPL/NASA; 27T, © NASA/NASA; 27ML, © JPL/NASA; 27MR, © Alejo Miranda/Shutterstock; 27B, © JPL/NASA; 28T, © Sputnik/Science Photo Library; 28BL, © AlexanderMokletsov/RIANovosti/AlexanderMokletsov/RIANovosti; 28BR, © NASA/NASA; 29T, © stockphoto mania/Shutterstock; 29B, © NASA/NASA; 30T, © Mechanik/Shutterstock; 30B, © 3Dsculptor/Shutterstock; 31L, © NASA/NASA; 31TR, © NASA/NASA; 31MR, © NASA/NASA; 31BR, © Castleski/NASA/Shutterstock; 32T, © Carlos Clarivan/Science Photo Library; 32B, © NASA/NASA; 33, © Digital Images Studio/NASA/Shutterstock; 34T, © NASA/NASA; 34B, © ESA/NASA; 35, © NASA/S.Dupuis/Alamy Stock; 36T, © Ken Ulbrich/NASA; 36B, © Adrian Mann/Stocktrek Images/Alamy Stock; 37T, © Oranzy Photography/NASA/Shutterstock; 37M, © FotograFFF/Shutterstock; 37B, © NASA/NASA; 38C, © NASA/NASA; 38BR, © Human Systems Engineering and Development Division/NASA; 39, © Marc Ward/Shutterstock; 40, © UPI/Alamy Stock; 41, © Geopix/Alamy Stock; 41TR, © ASSOCIATED PRESS; 41, © Marc Ward/Shutterstock; 42-43, © Warpaint/Shutterstock; 44BR, © Marshall Space Flight Center/NASA; 45T, © FotograFFF/Shutterstock; 45BR, © 3d-man/Shutterstock; 47, © phonlamaiphoto/Adobe Stock

Bearport Publishing Company Product Development Team

President: Jen Jenson; Director of Product Development: Spencer Brinker; Managing Editor: Allison Juda; Associate Editor: Naomi Reich; Associate Editor: Tiana Tran; Art Director: Colin O'Dea; Designer: Kim Jones; Designer: Kayla Eggert; Product Development Assistant: Owen Hamlin

Statement on Usage of Generative Artificial Intelligence

Bearport Publishing remains committed to publishing high-quality nonfiction books. Therefore, we restrict the use of generative AI to ensure accuracy of all text and visual components pertaining to a book's subject. See BearportPublishing.com for details.

Library of Congress Cataloging-in-Publication Data is available at www.loc.gov or upon request from the publisher.

ISBN: 979-8-89232-080-1 (hardcover)
ISBN: 979-8-89232-612-4 (paperback)
ISBN: 979-8-89232-213-3 (ebook)

© 2025 Arcturus Holdings Limited
This edition is published by arrangement with Arcturus Publishing Limited.

North American adaptations © 2025 Bearport Publishing Company. All rights reserved. No part of this publication may be reproduced in whole or in part, stored in any retrieval system, or transmitted in any form or by any means, electronic, mechanical, photocopying, recording, or otherwise, without written permission from the publisher. Bearport Publishing is a division of Chrysalis Education Group.

For more information, write to Bearport Publishing, 5357 Penn Avenue South, Minneapolis, MN 55419.

CONTENTS

Beyond Earth 4

Watching the Sky 6

Astronomers 8

Constellations 10

Comets............................... 12

Star Charts........................... 14

Optical Telescopes 16

The Chandra X-Ray Observatory 18

The James Webb Space Telescope....... 20

Eye of the Sky 22

Exploring Space 24

Space Probes 26

Astronauts 28

Crewed Spacecraft.................... 30

Apollo 11 32

The International Space Station 34

Spaceplanes 36

Mission to Mars 38

Space Tourism......................... 40

What Lies Beyond?.................... 42

Review and Reflect 44

Glossary............................. 46

Read More........................... 47

Learn More Online.................... 47

Index................................ 48

BEYOND EARTH

Space exploration did not begin with the rocket. It did not even begin with the telescope. Ever since the earliest humans gazed up at the night sky, we have been exploring outer space and learning about what exists beyond our planet.

Without advanced optical instruments or powerful machinery, early human space exploration was limited to observation. People carefully studied the movements, cycles, and phases of the sun, moon, and stars in an attempt to understand what they were seeing in the night sky and how it worked. Soon after humans invented the first writing systems, they began making star charts and catalogs. They recorded descriptions of eclipses, comets, meteors, and planetary movements.

With the invention of the telescope in 1608, space observation and exploration took a great leap forward. Astronomers soon confirmed that the sun was the center of our solar system, not Earth. This forever shifted the way we view our own importance and the place Earth occupies within the increasingly vast cosmos. But it was the development of the rocket in the early 20th century that would eventually allow us to leave our home planet behind and experience firsthand what lies beyond. In 1961, Yuri Gagarin became the first person to orbit Earth. Eight years later, astronauts Edwin "Buzz" Aldrin and Neil Armstrong walked on the moon, famously declaring it "one small step for a man, one giant leap for mankind."

We soon turned our attention toward exploring outer space. By looking upward and outward, we can learn about how our universe first burst into being and how it birthed all that we now see.

The Nebra Sky Disk is a bronze artifact possibly dating to 1800 BCE. It shows how early humans struggled to make sense of the skies. The disk depicts a full moon, a crescent moon, and the Pleiades star cluster.

Aldrin explored the surface of the moon after the **Apollo 11** landing. This photo was taken by mission commander Armstrong.

WATCHING THE SKY

Humans have always watched the night sky. At first, we believed the stars and planets were gods. We believed Earth was still while everything else in space moved around us. It took thousands of years to develop the mathematics and technology to begin to understand the universe.

To someone looking at the night sky from Earth, the stars and planets may appear to be fixed in the sky as though they are stuck onto the inner surface of a ball. Astronomers call this ball the celestial sphere. Although the celestial sphere is imaginary, it is a useful idea for astronomers because it can help them give coordinates for any object in the night sky.

When watching the night sky, it seems as if the stars rotate around us once a day. In fact, this apparent motion is caused by Earth's daily rotation on its own axis. Over the course of a year, the sun seems to move along a path, called the ecliptic, in front of a background of stars. This is actually caused by Earth's yearly rotation around the sun.

The planets also stay on the ecliptic, because they are all orbiting the sun along the same plane relative to Earth. Unlike the sun, however, the planets do not always move in the same direction along the ecliptic. Mercury and Venus are closer to the sun than Earth, so they orbit it more quickly. From Earth we see their orbits around the sun appear to move sometimes in the same direction and sometimes the opposite. The other planets orbit more slowly than Earth. When Earth is between one of these planets and the sun, we see the planet appear to go backward because we are moving faster.

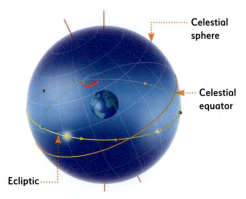

In this diagram of the celestial sphere, the ecliptic is shown in yellow. The ecliptic is tilted away from the equator, or mid-line, of the celestial sphere because Earth's axis is slightly tilted.

Naming and Numbering

Astronomers have developed many systems for naming objects in the sky. One of the most common comes from the New General Catalogue of Nebulae and Clusters of Stars, compiled by John Louis Emil Dreyer in 1888. It gives a number to 7,840 galaxies, star clusters, and nebulae. Another system is based on the Messier list of 110 objects, giving each a number with an M before it

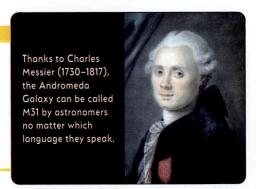

Thanks to Charles Messier (1730–1817), the Andromeda Galaxy can be called M31 by astronomers no matter which language they speak.

Taken over several hours, this photograph shows the stars' apparent nightly movement. On the equator, the stars rise in the east and set in the west. Farther away from the equator (as pictured), stars rise and set at an angle to the horizon.

ASTRONOMERS

In ancient civilizations from Babylon to India and from China to Central America, the earliest astronomers were often priests. As they studied movements in the night sky, they also searched for signs from the gods. While today's astronomers are scientists who observe, calculate, and test, they still find mysteries to be solved.

More than 3,000 years ago, Babylonian astronomers observed the movements of the sun and moon. They then used mathematics to create calendars to guide farmers over the year. In ancient Greece, beginning in the 4th century BCE, astronomers started to use geometry to work out the circumference of Earth and the distances to the sun and moon.

Babylonian calendar
The Babylonian sun god Shamash holds a coiled rope and a measuring rod.

The calendar's writing gives the time when three stars rise in each month.

Abd al-Rahman al-Sufi
The Persian astronomer al-Sufi (903–986 CE) published a book containing maps of 48 star constellations.

In ancient Greece, astronomers believed Earth was stationary at the center of the universe and that all other objects moved around it. One of the first to suggest that this idea was wrong was the Polish astronomer Nicolaus Copernicus, who used studies of planetary movements to prove that the sun was at the center of the solar system. This was the start of using the scientific method in astronomy. It began to include careful observations leading to theories, which were then tested by more observations. Using the scientific method and mathematics, Albert Einstein predicted black holes in 1915. It was not until 2019 that astronomers were able to photograph one.

Nicolaus Copernicus

Nicolaus Copernicus (1473–1543) developed the theory that Earth moves around the sun. It took more than a century for his theory to be widely accepted.

Caroline Herschel

The first woman to receive a salary as a scientist, German astronomer Caroline Herschel (1750–1848), discovered several comets.

Albert Einstein

Albert Einstein (1879–1955) used mathematics to reveal the relationships between space, time, and the structure of the universe.

Nancy Roman

As Chief of Astronomy at the National Aeronautics and Space Administration (NASA), Nancy Roman (1925–2018) planned the Hubble Space Telescope, which helped calculate the age of the universe.

CONSTELLATIONS

A constellation is a group of stars that appears to form the pattern of a person, animal, or object. Today's astronomers recognize 88 official constellations, including 48 that were named after figures from myths in ancient Greece. Well-known patterns within constellations, such as the Big Dipper, are called asterisms.

Referencing the constellations is a useful way for astronomers to describe the location of an object, such as a galaxy, that appears to lie within them. There are several methods for identifying the stars in a constellation, including the Bayer system, which gives each star a letter from the Greek or Latin alphabet, to help distinguish brightness.

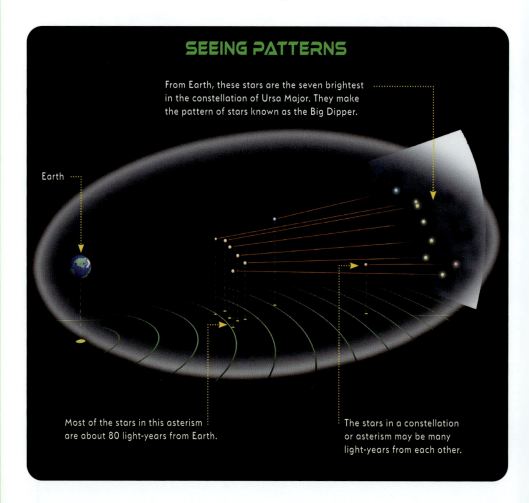

SEEING PATTERNS

From Earth, these stars are the seven brightest in the constellation of Ursa Major. They make the pattern of stars known as the Big Dipper.

Earth

Most of the stars in this asterism are about 80 light-years from Earth.

The stars in a constellation or asterism may be many light-years from each other.

Through the year, the sun seems to pass through 12 constellations along the ecliptic. These are known as the constellations of the zodiac.

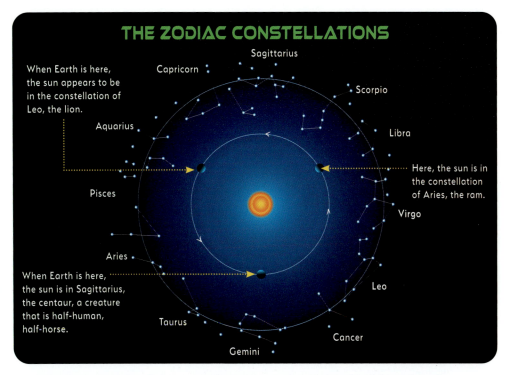

The North Star, also known as Polaris, lies at the north pole of the celestial sphere, making it useful to find north at night. The North Star is the brightest star in the constellation of Ursa Minor, Little Bear. The South Star, also known as Polaris Australis, is in the constellation of Octans, but its faintness makes it difficult to spot.

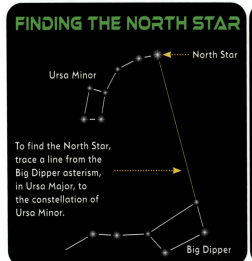

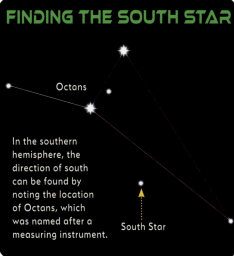

COMETS

Comets are small, icy objects that travel inside our solar system with very stretched, elliptical orbits that take them both close to and far from the sun. When comets get near the sun, they get hot and release gases. In most years, at least one comet can be seen from Earth with the naked eye, while several more can be spotted with a telescope.

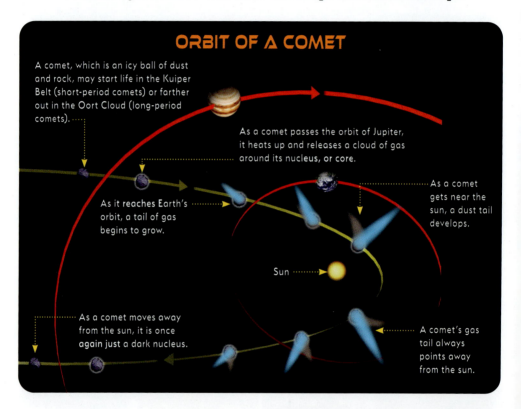

ORBIT OF A COMET

A comet, which is an icy ball of dust and rock, may start life in the Kuiper Belt (short-period comets) or farther out in the Oort Cloud (long-period comets).

As a comet passes the orbit of Jupiter, it heats up and releases a cloud of gas around its nucleus, or core.

As it reaches Earth's orbit, a tail of gas begins to grow.

As a comet gets near the sun, a dust tail develops.

Sun

As a comet moves away from the sun, it is once again just a dark nucleus.

A comet's gas tail always points away from the sun.

Halley's Comet

Type: Short-period comet
Size of nucleus: 6.8 miles (11 km) across
Speed when closest to the sun: 122,000 miles per hour (196,000 kph)
Speed when farthest from the sun: 2,000 mph (3,200 kph)
Length of orbit: 75 years
Next pass near Earth: 2061

Halley's Comet was seen from England in 1066, as shown in the Bayeux Tapestry

Comet Wild 2

Wild (VILT) 2 is a comet visible from Earth every 6 years.

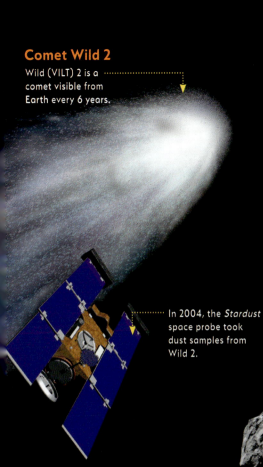

In 2004, the *Stardust* space probe took dust samples from Wild 2.

Halley's Comet

This infrared image shows the different temperatures of the comet's nucleus and tails.

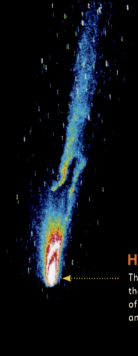

Churyumov–Gerasimenko

This photograph was taken by the *Rosetta* space probe, which landed on the 3.7-mile- (6-km-) wide comet in 2014.

The gas tail glows blue.

Comet Hale-Bopp

The long-period comet Hale-Bopp was visible to the naked eye in 1997 but will not pass Earth again until 4385.

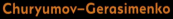

The dust tail is made of grit from the comet's nucleus.

13

STAR CHARTS

These star charts show the constellations of the northern and southern celestial hemispheres. Earth's movement around the sun means that not every constellation in a hemisphere can be viewed all year from every location. Because of Earth's rotation, the stars rotate around the north and south celestial poles once a day.

NORTHERN HEMISPHERE

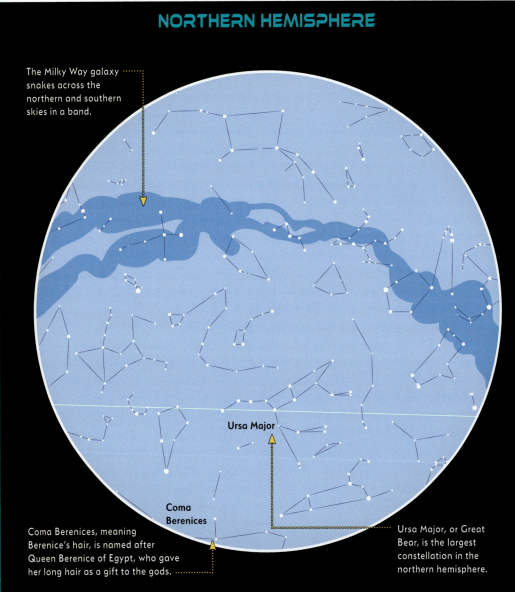

The Milky Way galaxy snakes across the northern and southern skies in a band.

Ursa Major

Coma Berenices

Coma Berenices, meaning Berenice's hair, is named after Queen Berenice of Egypt, who gave her long hair as a gift to the gods.

Ursa Major, or Great Bear, is the largest constellation in the northern hemisphere.

The northern constellations are found in the northern hemisphere of the celestial sphere above the celestial equator. Most of the 36 modern northern constellations are based on those described by the ancient Greeks, which may have their roots in Babylonian astronomy from thousands of years earlier.

There are 52 southern constellations. Most of the southern constellations are in regions of the sky not viewable from Europe, so they were not mapped by the ancient Greeks. Many were mapped from the 16th century, when European sailors journeyed south of the equator, although peoples of the southern hemisphere had long had their own names and stories about the stars.

SOUTHERN HEMISPHERE

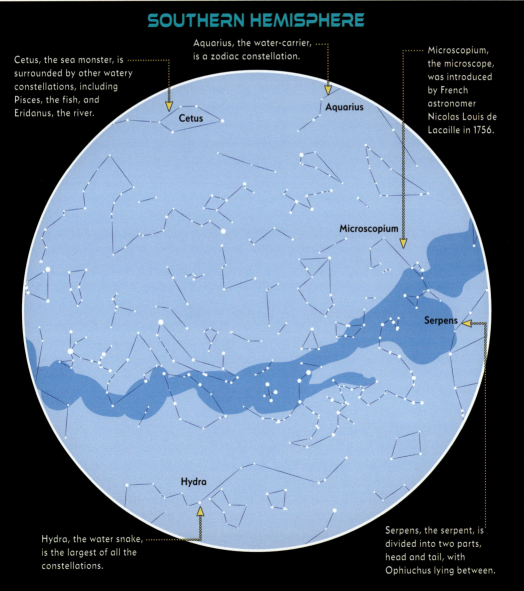

Cetus, the sea monster, is surrounded by other watery constellations, including Pisces, the fish, and Eridanus, the river.

Aquarius, the water-carrier, is a zodiac constellation.

Microscopium, the microscope, was introduced by French astronomer Nicolas Louis de Lacaille in 1756.

Serpens, the serpent, is divided into two parts, head and tail, with Ophiuchus lying between.

Hydra, the water snake, is the largest of all the constellations.

15

OPTICAL TELESCOPES

An optical telescope gathers and focuses visible light to create a brighter and magnified image, which lets us see distant objects more clearly. Visible light is the light we see with our own eyes. The telescope was invented in 1608 by spectacle-maker Hans Lippershey and enabled great leaps forward in astronomy.

REFRACTING TELESCOPE

The earliest telescopes were refracting telescopes.

A second lens acts like a magnifying glass, making the image bigger.

The objective lens refracts, or bends, light rays.

The objective lens is a piece of glass that is convex, meaning its surface curves outward. This lets it gather more light than the human eye could collect on its own.

The distance from the objective lens to the point where the light is focused is called the focal length. A longer focal length increases magnification.

Galileo's refracting telescope

In 1609, Italian astronomer Galileo Galilei improved on Hans Lippershey's invention and was the first to use a telescope for astronomy.

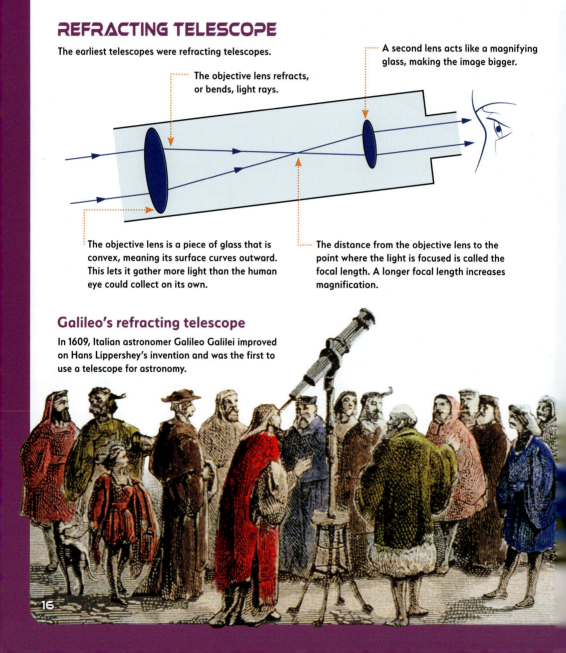

REFLECTING TELESCOPE

The first reflecting telescope, more powerful than a refracting telescope, was built by English astronomer Sir Isaac Newton in 1668.

The wide primary mirror has a concave, or inward-curving, surface. This gathers lots of light and reflects it onto the secondary mirror.

The flat secondary mirror reflects the light into the eyepiece.

The light is focused, forming an image.

A lens in the eyepiece magnifies the image.

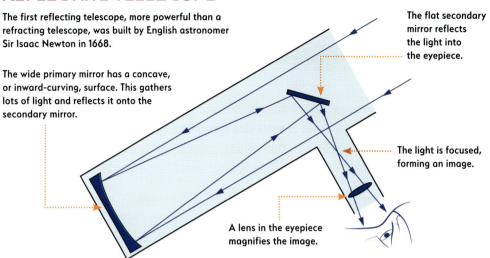

GRAN TELESCOPIO CANARIAS

The world's largest optical telescope is in the Canary Islands, Spain.

The main mirror, made up of 36 hexagonal segments, collects light from the night sky.

The light is reflected to a second mirror, which in turn reflects onto a series of other mirrors, creating a long focal length.

The telescope swivels and turns to focus on any point in the sky.

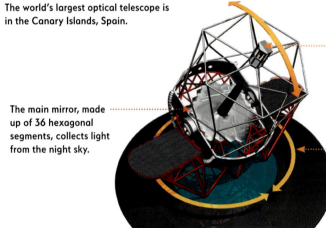

Gran Telescopio Canarias

Type: Optical reflecting telescope
Size of main mirror: 34.1 feet (10.4 m) across
Focal length: 557.5 ft. (169.9 m)
Completed: 2007
Built by: Scientific organizations in Spain, Mexico, and the United States

The telescope is 7,438 ft. (2,267 m) above sea level. This helps it avoid any light pollution from below.

THE CHANDRA X-RAY OBSERVATORY

Chandra is a telescope that records X-rays, a form of energy invisible to the human eye. Since most X-rays are absorbed by Earth's atmosphere, Chandra is on a satellite that orbits in space. The telescope is named after the astronomer Subrahmanyan Chandrasekhar.

Visible light is just one form of energy given off by stars, black holes, and other objects. The whole range of energy is called the electromagnetic spectrum. This energy travels through space in waves. When studying the waves, we can note their wavelength, or the distance between the peak of one wave and the next.

Visible light is in the middle of the electromagnetic spectrum. Its wavelengths are shorter than radio waves but longer than X-rays. Stars give off most of their energy as visible light. Long wavelengths—radio waves, microwaves, and infrared—have the lowest energy. They come from the coolest, darkest regions of space. At the other end of the spectrum are X-rays and gamma rays, which have very high energy. X-rays come from superhot spinning neutron stars and from the material circling black holes.

Chandra uses mirrors to direct X-rays through grating containing thousands of narrow openings. This divides the rays by wavelength. A detector then records the position of each X-ray and its energy level. Together, this builds up a picture of the object emitting X-rays.

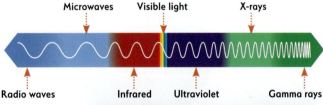

Visible light is in the middle of the electromagnetic spectrum. It is made up of all the colors of the rainbow.

Chandra X-Ray Observatory

Type: X-ray space telescope
Size of main mirror: 3.9 ft. (1.2 m) across
Focal length: 32.8 ft. (10 m)
Average distance from Earth: 50,000 miles (80,000 km)
Launch: 1999
Built by: NASA and other U.S. organizations

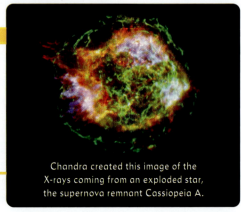

Chandra created this image of the X-rays coming from an exploded star, the supernova remnant Cassiopeia A.

THE JAMES WEBB SPACE TELESCOPE

Launched in 2021, the James Webb Space Telescope observes the universe in visible light as well as infrared. It was intended to replace the Hubble Space Telescope, launched in 1990. The Webb Telescope is able to see much more distant objects. It was named after the NASA administrator who oversaw the United States' earliest spaceflights.

When objects are very distant, their light is stretched to a longer wavelength as it travels toward us. This means energy that began as visible light appears as infrared or radio waves by the time it reaches us. By observing infrared, the Webb Telescope is able to see some of the most distant objects in the universe. Since they are so distant, their light has taken billions of years to reach the telescope. As a result, the telescope is capturing images that show what was happening in the earliest days of the universe, including the formation of the first galaxies.

Infrared can be felt as heat, and therefore the Webb Telescope needs to be kept very cold to avoid damage. The telescope has its own sunshade to keep its instruments below -370 degrees Fahrenheit (-223 degrees Celsius). In addition, the Webb Telescope actually orbits the sun rather than Earth, but it stays in Earth's shadow at all times.

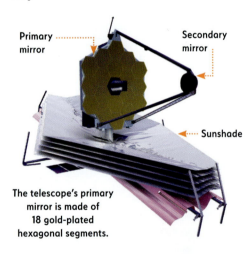

The telescope's primary mirror is made of 18 gold-plated hexagonal segments.

James Webb Space Telescope

Type: Infrared and optical space telescope
Size of main mirror: 21 ft. (6.4 m) across
Focal length: 431 ft. (131 m)
Average distance from Earth: 930,000 miles (1.5 million km)
Launch: 2021
Built by: NASA, European Space Agency (ESA), and Canadian Space Agency (CSA)

Engineers clean the telescope's secondary mirror

Scientists examine the segments of the James Webb Telescope's main mirror before launch.

EYE OF THE SKY

Eye of the Sky, officially known as FAST (Five-hundred-meter Aperture Spherical radio Telescope), was built into the hills of Guizhou, China. Its 1,600-foot- (500-m-) wide bowl-shaped dish is the largest of its type. It gathers radio waves from objects such as pulsars, which are the spinning cores of collapsed supergiant stars.

The dish of a radio telescope acts in a way similar to the mirror in a reflecting telescope. It reflects and focuses radio waves onto a device called a receiving antenna. FAST's receiver hangs 459 ft. (140 m) above the dish, giving a focal length of the same distance. The receiver amplifies, or increases, the radio waves, which are recorded so they can be studied on a computer.

Since the radio waves from distant objects are very weak, large dishes are needed to collect enough radio energy to study them. Radio telescopes are located far from cities and towns, so radios and other electronic devices cannot interfere.

The FAST dish cannot turn to face any point in the sky like smaller radio telescopes. Instead, it is fixed in a natural valley. However, the dish is made of 4,450 triangular metal panels that can be tilted to face particular objects, as long as they are not too low in the horizon.

Smaller, movable radio telescopes use the same principles as FAST but are often placed in groups that work together.

Eye of the Sky (FAST)

Type: Radio telescope
Size of dish: 1,600 ft. (500 m) across
Focal length: 460 ft. (140 m)
Completed: 2016
Built by: Chinese National Astronomical Observatories (NAOC) and Chinese Academy of Sciences

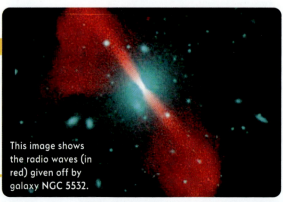

This image shows the radio waves (in red) given off by galaxy NGC 5532.

In 2017, just one year after starting work, Eye of the Sky discovered two new pulsars. They were named FAST pulsars #1 and #2.

EXPLORING SPACE

The first human-made object in space was the Soviet Union's uncrewed *Sputnik 1* satellite, which orbited Earth in 1957. Since then, humans have walked on our moon and sent uncrewed space probes to planets, moons, and comets in the distant solar system.

The dividing line between Earth's atmosphere and outer space is considered to be 62 miles (100 km) above Earth's surface. To explore space, humans had to build vehicles that could overcome the pull of Earth's gravity, the force that constantly pulls us to the ground. By the middle of the 20th century, engineers had designed rockets powerful enough to lift spacecraft into space. Rockets push out superhot gas that sends them upward at high speed. When a rocket has lifted its spacecraft high enough, the rocket detaches and falls back to Earth.

For a spacecraft to escape Earth's gravity and fly into space, it must reach a speed of 25,039 mph (40,296 kph). This is known as the escape velocity. Once in space, satellites do not need to travel as fast. A satellite only needs to balance Earth's gravity rather than escape it. To orbit at 125 miles (200 km) above Earth's surface, for example, the speed needed is 17,025 mph (27,400 kph). Once a satellite reaches this speed with the help of a rocket, it can continue in a curved path, circling Earth and firing its own engines only to correct its course.

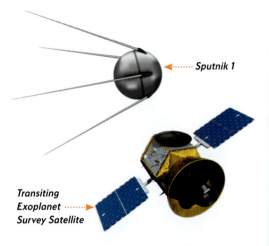

Sputnik 1

Transiting Exoplanet Survey Satellite

Sputnik 1 lasted only 5 months in orbit. Today, there are almost 10,000 active satellites in Earth's orbit, including the *Exoplanet Survey*, which looks for exoplanets.

Astrodynamics

Astrodynamics is the study of how rockets and spacecraft move through space as they fire their engines and are pulled by the gravity of stars and planets. Astrodynamics is based on mathematical equations about motion, including the fact that a moving object will keep moving unless another force acts upon it. Mathematician Katherine Johnson did the astrodynamics calculations that made the United States' first crewed spaceflights possible.

Katherine Johnson (1918–2020) made flight path calculations for NASA.

Astronaut Randy Bresnik performs a space walk as he works on one of the International Space Station's robotic arms.

SPACE PROBES

Space probes are uncrewed robotic spacecraft that travel where humans cannot currently go because the journey or destination is too dangerous or too distant. Space probes can fly by, orbit, or land on planets, moons, comets, and asteroids. They can even journey beyond the solar system.

BepiColombo

Launched in 2018, *BepiColombo* is a joint European and Japanese mission to Mercury. It should reach the planet in 2025.

Once at Mercury, the magnetospheric orbiter will separate to observe the planet's magnetic field.

The planetary orbiter will study Mercury's rocks and craters.

The probe travels through space using power from its solar panels. It is helped along by the gravity of Earth and Venus, which pull the probe ahead.

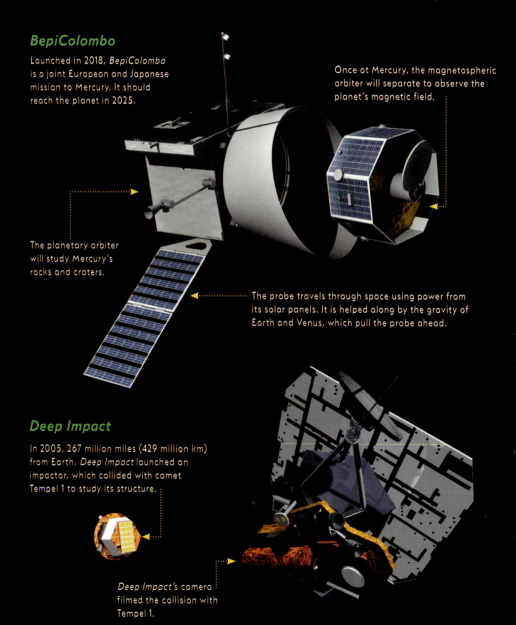

Deep Impact

In 2005, 267 million miles (429 million km) from Earth, *Deep Impact* launched an impactor, which collided with comet Tempel 1 to study its structure.

Deep Impact's camera filmed the collision with Tempel 1.

Galileo

In 1995, *Galileo* was the first spacecraft to orbit Jupiter and study its moons.

The radio antenna was 16 ft. (4.9 m) wide.

Generators made electricity from the heat released by the radioactive element plutonium.

Voyager 1

Voyager 1 is the most distant human-made object. It left the heliosphere, or region surrounding the sun in the solar system, in 2012.

Voyager 1's radio antenna sends information to Earth and receives commands using radio waves.

Chang'e 4

In 2019, this Chinese probe made the first soft landing on the far side of the moon.

Voyager 1

Type: Mariner Jupiter-Saturn space probe
Equipment: Cameras, plus instruments for studying magnetic fields, plasma, and cosmic rays
Size: 1.5 x 5.8 ft. (0.5 x 1.8 m) main body
Engines: 16 thrusters
Rocket: Titan IIIE-Centaur
Launch date: September 5, 1977
Operator: NASA

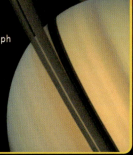

In 1996, *Voyager 1* took this photograph of Saturn and its moons Tethys and Dione.

ASTRONAUTS

Astronauts are the crew members and pilots of spacecraft. The United States and the Soviet Union were the first countries to send astronauts into space beginning in the early 1960s. It was not until 1978 that a citizen of another country reached space. Today, more than 550 people from more than 40 countries have made the journey.

Early astronauts were often military fighter pilots, who had already proven their bravery and quick thinking. Today, crew members are also scientists, doctors, or teachers who perform experiments in space. Until 2002, astronauts were trained and paid only by governments. Since then, some astronauts have been employed by businesses to pilot their spacecraft, such as Crew Dragon. In 2001, millionaire Dennis Tito became the first space tourist after he paid to stay on the International Space Station (ISS) for eight days.

Yuri Gagarin

Soviet astronaut Yuri Gagarin (1934–1968) was the first human in space. He traveled on *Vostok 1*.

Valentina Tereshkova

In 1963, Soviet astronaut Valentina Tereshkova (born 1937) became the first woman in space. She orbited Earth 48 times alone on *Vostok 6*.

Mae Jemison

U.S. astronaut Mae Jemison (born 1956) was the first Black American woman in space, serving as a Mission Specialist on board Space Shuttle *Endeavour* in 1992.

During a space walk, an astronaut wears a space suit called an Extravehicular Mobility Unit (EMU), which is attached by a tether to the spacecraft. An EMU is equipped with an oxygen supply, since there is no air to breathe in space. The suit protects the astronaut from extreme temperatures, which range from -247°F (-155°C) in the shade to 248°F (120°C) in sunlight. The EMU also keeps out harmful radiation from the sun, as well as space dust, which can travel as fast as a bullet. During takeoff and landing, a lighter suit and helmet are worn, designed to keep the astronaut safe during changes in temperature and pressure.

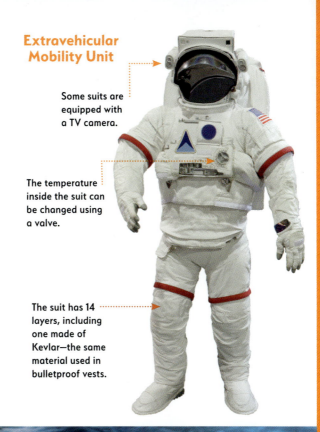

Extravehicular Mobility Unit

Some suits are equipped with a TV camera.

The temperature inside the suit can be changed using a valve.

The suit has 14 layers, including one made of Kevlar—the same material used in bulletproof vests.

Emergency training
U.S. astronaut Franklin Chang Díaz (born 1950) floats in a life raft during a training exercise. He and other astronauts were practicing exiting a malfunctioning Space Shuttle over the ocean.

CREWED SPACECRAFT

Crewed spacecraft have never journeyed farther than Earth's moon. Aside from spaceplanes, most crewed spacecraft are space capsules that are launched into Earth's orbit by a rocket. After completing their mission, the crew descends in a wingless reentry capsule, which lands in an ocean or desert. Its descent is slowed by parachutes and sometimes by engines.

Vostok

Launched by a Vostok-K rocket, a Vostok space capsule carried Yuri Gagarin on a single Earth orbit in 1961.

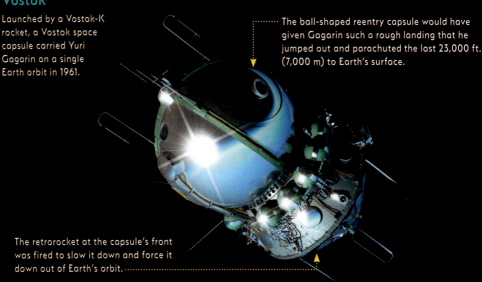

The ball-shaped reentry capsule would have given Gagarin such a rough landing that he jumped out and parachuted the last 23,000 ft. (7,000 m) to Earth's surface.

The retrorocket at the capsule's front was fired to slow it down and force it down out of Earth's orbit.

Soyuz

First launched by the Soviet Union in 1966, Soyuz capsules have made more than 140 flights.

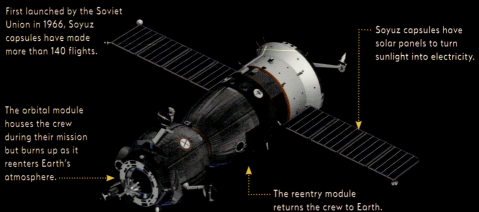

Soyuz capsules have solar panels to turn sunlight into electricity.

The orbital module houses the crew during their mission but burns up as it reenters Earth's atmosphere.

The reentry module returns the crew to Earth.

30

Mercury

The launch escape system carried three rockets that could be fired in an emergency to push the capsule away from its rocket.

Gemini

This illustration shows the interior of the adapter module, which carried four spherical retrorockets.

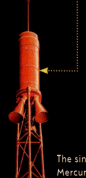

The single-person Mercury crew compartment carried the first American into space, Alan Shepard, in 1961.

During 1965 and 1966, 10 two-astronaut crews orbited Earth in NASA's Gemini capsules.

Crew Dragon

Crew Dragon's nose cone opens to reveal its docking mechanism used to connect to the ISS.

Crew Dragon

Type: Partly reusable space capsule
Seats: 7
Size: 27 x 13 ft. (8 x 4 m)
Engines: 16 Draco thrusters
Rocket: Falcon 9 Block 5
Launch date: May 30, 2020
Operator: SpaceX Corp

Crew Dragon launches on top of a Falcon 9 rocket at NASA's Kennedy Space Center in Florida

APOLLO 11

On July 20, 1969, the Apollo 11 mission landed U.S. astronauts Neil Armstrong and Edwin "Buzz" Aldrin on the moon, while Michael Collins waited for them on board their command and service module in orbit. Armstrong and Aldrin were the first and second humans to set foot on the moon.

The United States' Apollo missions began in 1967 with the aim of putting the first humans on Earth's moon. It was only in 1961 that the Soviet Union had sent the first human into space. Apollo 10, the mission before Apollo 11, had been a practice run for the moon landing, successfully orbiting the moon in May 1969.

The Apollo spacecraft had three parts: a command module containing the astronauts' cabin, a service module holding the engine, and a lunar module for landing on the moon. The mission began on July 16 when the spacecraft carrying the three astronauts was blasted into Earth's orbit by a Saturn V rocket.

Around two hours after leaving Earth, the rocket had done its work. It left Apollo to fly into the moon's orbit alone. On July 20, Armstrong and Aldrin undocked the lunar module from the command and service module and flew down to the moon's surface. The astronauts spent 21 hours and 36 minutes on the moon, taking photographs, doing experiments, and choosing rock samples.

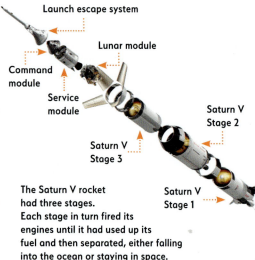

The Saturn V rocket had three stages. Each stage in turn fired its engines until it had used up its fuel and then separated, either falling into the ocean or staying in space.

Apollo 11

Type: Crewed moon landing mission
Spacecraft: Apollo command and service module *Columbia* and Apollo lunar module *Eagle*
Rocket: Saturn V
Launch date: July 16, 1969
Landing site: Sea of Tranquility
End of mission: July 24, 1969
Operator: NASA

After having left the lunar module to crash into the moon and the service module to burn up, the command module splashed down in the Pacific Ocean on July 24.

THE INTERNATIONAL SPACE STATION

The ISS orbits Earth from about 255 miles (410 km) away. A space station is a human-made satellite in which astronauts live for an extended period of time. On the ISS, the astronauts do astronomy and weather experiments, as well as studying what happens to living things in space.

The ISS was put together module by module while in orbit, starting in 1998. To carry out this construction, astronauts did more than 1,000 hours of space walks, working outside the safety of a spacecraft. They were helped by a large robotic arm called Canadarm2.

The ISS has been continually occupied since 2000, with different astronauts staying for a few weeks or months at a time. After the retirement of the U.S. Space Shuttles in 2011, Russian Soyuz spacecraft were the only way for astronauts to get to and from the space station until Crew Dragon began its flights in 2020.

The ISS has a microgravity environment, which means the pull of gravity is felt very little. Astronauts float around inside the ISS. Earth's gravity is actually pulling on the space station and the astronauts almost as strongly as if they were on Earth. But since they are all falling together and at the same rate, the astronauts appear to float.

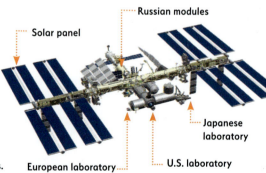

One section of the ISS is operated by Russia, while the rest is shared by astronauts from many countries.

International Space Station

Type: Modular space station
Crew: Up to 6 astronauts
Size: 358 x 239 ft. (109 x 73 m)
Daily orbits of Earth: 15.5
Launch date: November 20, 1998
Operators: NASA, ESA, CSA, Russian State Space Corporation (Roscosmos), and Japan Aerospace Exploration Agency (JAXA)

ESA astronaut Samantha Cristoforetti works with science equipment on board the ISS.

34

NASA astronaut Chris Cassidy photographs Earth from the ISS's Cupola module, built by the European Space Agency.

SPACEPLANES

Like space capsules, spaceplanes are launched into space by rockets that drop away after use. However, spaceplanes have wings so they can fly back down to Earth on their own. Spaceplanes remain in a low orbit around Earth. The U.S. Space Shuttle was the most successful spaceplane.

Dream Chaser

Currently in development, Dream Chaser will carry cargo or crew to the ISS.

Dream Chaser will launch vertically on an Ariane 5 or Vulcan Centaur rocket, but it will land horizontally on an ordinary runway.

Boeing X-37

The Boeing X-37 is a robotic, uncrewed spaceplane that first flew missions for the U.S. Air Force in 2010.

While in orbit, the X-37 unfolds a solar panel to make electricity from sunlight.

Space Shuttle

The engines were used both during launch and while in orbital flight.

Endeavour was one of five Space Shuttles in operation.

The cargo bay carried satellites and ISS modules.

The flight deck held the crew's compartment.

Buran

Buran was a Soviet spaceplane that made only one uncrewed flight in 1988 before being discontinued due to costs.

The Buran spaceplane was launched by a 5,300,000-pound (2,400,000-kg) Energia rocket.

With a solid rocket booster on either side, Space Shuttle *Endeavour* lifts off attached to its fuel tank (red). The boosters and tank were dropped after launch.

Space Shuttle

Type: Partly reusable low-Earth orbital spaceplane
Seats: Up to 8
Size: 78 ft. (24 m) across wings
Engines: 3 RS-25s
Rocket: 2 reusable solid rocket boosters
Launch date: April 12, 1981
Retirement: July 21, 2011
Operator: NASA

MISSION TO MARS

Humans have never set foot on another planet, but the Russian, European, and United States space agencies all have plans to send people to Mars. Before they can realize this dream, they must build a rocket that could be transported to Mars and then launch from the surface of the Red Planet for the return journey to Earth.

NASA has the most advanced plans to send humans to Mars. They hope to make the trip during the 2030s. NASA is working on a spacecraft, *Orion*, that would make the long journey. It will have the same basic structure as the Apollo spacecraft but will be larger and stronger. It will also be powered by solar panels while in space and could be inhabited for a year. *Orion* could be docked with a habitation module, which could be held in Mars's orbit in a similar way to the ISS.

Scientists are also developing technologies to allow humans to live on the surface of Mars by using the planet's own resources to make water and oxygen. Water could be extracted and gathered from the soil of the planet. Oxygen could be made by splitting water into its parts—oxygen and hydrogen. Fuel to power a rocket for the return journey would be too heavy to carry to Mars. But all the ingredients for fuel—oxygen, hydrogen, and carbon—can be found on Mars itself.

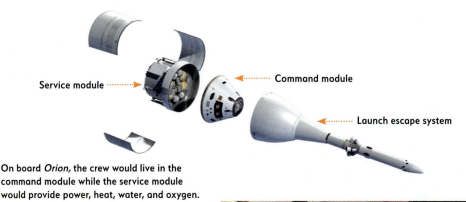

On board *Orion*, the crew would live in the command module while the service module would provide power, heat, water, and oxygen.

NASA Mission to Mars

Type: Crewed Mars landing mission
Spacecraft: *Orion*
Rocket: Space Launch System rocket
Launch date: 2030s
Length of journey: 7 months to reach Mars
Operator: NASA

This NASA illustration imagines an astronaut growing plants in a greenhouse to provide food on Mars.

It would take at least five spacecraft to carry all the equipment needed to live on Mars: rovers, living modules, and support modules.

SPACE TOURISM

It used to be that the only people who flew into space were highly skilled astronauts. Most of them had been military pilots who agreed to undergo extremely difficult physical and mental examinations—as well as years of exhausting training—before even being considered for a spaceflight crew. But times have changed, and now the opportunity for space exploration has been opened to others.

Today, ordinary people are able to make short trips beyond Earth's atmosphere as space tourists. In the first decade of the 21st century, 7 civilians became the first-ever space tourists, traveling on a Russian spacecraft to the ISS. Each paid about $25 million for their trip. At about the same time, private aerospace companies began offering other paying customers seats on craft flying about 60 miles (97 km) above Earth's surface. This is just beyond the Karman Line that separates Earth's atmosphere from outer space.

In the near future, space tourists will probably be able to pay to orbit the moon. Prices for seats on spacecraft are expected to eventually come down, putting space travel within reach for more people. Some companies are already planning ring-shaped hotels that will host guests as they orbit Earth. Others envision a future in which shuttles will regularly carry both colonists and tourists back and forth from Earth to settlements on other planets.

Citizens in Space

Space tourists are no longer confined to suborbital altitudes. In 2021, the private aerospace company SpaceX launched the Inspiration4 mission. It was the first human spaceflight to orbit Earth with a crew made up entirely of private citizens.

Passengers on Inspiration4, the world's first all-civilian mission to space, performed several science experiments and conducted video calls to Earth.

William Shatner (*second from left*) was an actor in the original Star Trek series. He took a real, 11-minute trip into space aboard a Blue Origin flight along with three other passengers. At age 90, Shatner became the oldest person ever to have flown in space.

WHAT LIES BEYOND?

Ever since the first person looked up at the twinkling lights in the night sky, we've had questions. What are those shining dots, and why do they move? What else is out there?

Today, humans continue to ask questions as they peer and probe ever deeper into space. The ISS is continuously staffed by scientists performing important medical, biological, and space research. Robotic rovers are combing the surface of Mars and the moon, collecting soil samples, mapping the terrain, and looking for signs of water that may indicate life. Unmanned space probes are orbiting, photographing, and collecting data on the other planets and moons in our solar system.

With space telescopes and supercomputers, humans can now see farther into space than ever before. But there will always be more questions to answer and other mysteries to solve. Someday in the distant future, we may be able to venture to other planets and other suns. We may even find a way to go beyond the Milky Way. No matter how far we travel or how much we learn, we will always gaze up at the starry night sky with a desire to know more.

REVIEW AND REFLECT

Now that you've read about the exploration of space, let's review what you've learned. Use the following questions to reflect on your newfound knowledge and integrate it with what you already knew.

Check for Understanding

1. How has the role of an astronomer changed over the last 3,000 years? *(See p. 8)*

2. Name a scientist who studied space or astronomy and describe what they did. *(See p. 9)*

3. What is a constellation? How does it relate to an asterism? *(See p. 10)*

4. What is a comet made of? How does a comet change as it travels through the solar system? *(See p. 12)*

5. Name a constellation and provide at least one detail about it. *(See pp. 14–15)*

6. What is one part of a telescope? What does that part do or how does it work? *(See pp. 16–17)*

7. Name three forms of energy in the electromagnetic spectrum. *(See pp. 18–19)*

8. What happens to light wavelengths as they travel long distances? *(See p. 20)*

9. Why does the dish of a radio telescope need to be big? *(See p. 22)*

10. What was the first human-made object in space? When was it launched? *(See pp. 24–25)*

11. How has the job of astronauts changed over time? How has astronaut training evolved? *(See pp. 28–29)*

12. Name a crewed spacecraft and describe one of its features. *(See pp. 30–31)*

13. What did Buzz Aldrin and Neil Armstrong do on the surface of the Moon in 1969? *(See p. 32)*

14. What is the International Space Station (ISS)? What happens there, and why is it important? *(See p. 34)*

15. What are two things that need to happen before humans can go to Mars? *(See p. 40)*

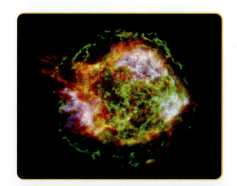

44

Making Connections

1. Choose two people mentioned in this book. In your own words, explain why each was important to the study of space.

2. Name a telescope discussed in the book. What is special about it?

3. What is a space probe? How is it similar to and different from crewed spacecraft?

4. What are some differences between what people understood about space before the invention of the telescope in 1608 and what we know now?

5. How are spaceplanes similar to space capsules? How are they different?

In Your Own Words

1. What can people on Earth learn from studying space? Why is it valuable or important?

2. What impact do you think the invention of the telescope had on astronomy or other branches of science?

3. For you personally, what would be the most challenging part of traveling in space?

4. Why do you think humans are interested in learning more about space? What do you think is most interesting about space?

5. How do you think space travel will change in the future?

GLOSSARY

asteroid a small rocky or metal object, more than 3 ft. (1 m) wide, that orbits the sun

astronomer a scientist who studies the objects in space

axis an imaginary line through a planet or moon, around which the object rotates

black hole an area of space with such strong gravity that no matter or light can escape from it

comet a small icy object with an elliptical orbit that takes it both close to and far from the sun

core the inner region of a planet or moon

day the time taken for a planet or moon to rotate on its axis until the sun appears to return to the same position in the sky

eclipse when a body such as a star, planet, or moon is obscured by passing into the shadow of another body or by having another body pass between it and the viewer

ecliptic the plane of Earth's orbit around the sun

exoplanet a planet outside our solar system

galaxy millions or billions of stars, as well as gas and dust, that are held together by gravity

hemisphere half of a sphere, such as that of a planet or moon

hydrogen the most common and lightest element in the universe; hydrogen is a gas at room temperature

infrared a type of energy, given off by objects, that humans can feel as heat

light-year the distance that light travels in 1 year: 5.88 trillion miles (9.46 trillion km)

nebula a cloud of gas and dust

orbit the curved path of an object around a star, planet, or moon

oxygen the third most common element in the universe; oxygen is a gas at room temperature and is essential for life

plasma an electrically charged gas made of free electrons and atoms that have lost electrons

radioactive relating to a substance that releases energy as its atoms decay

radio wave a type of energy, given off by objects, that can be used for communications

satellite a human-made object that is placed in orbit around a planet or moon

solar panel a device that turns sunlight into electricity

space probe an uncrewed spacecraft

ultraviolet a type of energy, given off by objects including the sun

wavelength the distance between the peaks of waves of energy

year the time taken for a planet to complete one orbit around the sun

READ MORE

Green, Joel. *Black Holes (Tech Bytes: Exploring Space).* Fairpoint, NY: Norwood House Press, 2023.

Hurt, Avery Elizabeth. *The Future of Space Exploration (Opposing Viewpoints).* New York: Greenhaven Publishing, 2020.

Mann, Dionna L. *Hidden Heroes in Space Exploration (Alternator Books. Who Else in History?).* Minneapolis: Lerner Publications, 2023.

Martin, Claudia. *The Solar System (Space Revealed).* Minneapolis: Bearport Publishing Company, 2025.

LEARN MORE ONLINE

1. Go to **www.factsurfer.com** or scan the QR code below.
2. Enter "**Space Exploration**" into the search box.
3. Click on the cover of this book to see a list of websites.

INDEX

Aldrin, Edwin "Buzz" 4–5, 32–33
al-Sufi, Abd al-Rahman 8
Andromeda Galaxy 6
Apollo missions 5, 32–33, 38
Armstrong, Neil 4–5, 32–33
asterisms 10–11
asteroids 26
astronauts 4, 28–29, 31–32, 34–35, 38, 40
Babylonian astronomy 8, 15
BepiColombo 26
black holes 9, 18
Boeing X-37 36
Buran 37
celestial sphere 6, 11, 15
comets 4, 9, 12–13, 24, 26
constellations 8, 10–11, 14–15
Copernicus, Nicolaus 9
Crew Dragon 28, 31, 34
Deep Impact 26
Dream Chaser 36
Earth 4, 6, 8–14, 18, 20, 24, 26–28, 30–32, 34–38, 40
eclipses 4
ecliptic 6, 11
Einstein, Albert 9
escape velocity 24
exoplanets 24
Gagarin, Yuri 4, 28, 30
galaxies 6, 10, 14, 20, 22
Galilei, Galileo 16
Gemini 11, 31
gravity 24, 26, 34
heliosphere 27
Herschel, Caroline 9
Hubble Space Telescope 9, 20
International Space Station 25, 28, 31, 34–38, 40, 42

James Webb Telescope 20–21
Jemison, Mae 28
Johnson, Katherine 24
Jupiter 12, 27
Kuiper Belt 12
life 12, 29, 42
light 10, 16–18, 20
Mariner probes 27
Mars 38–39, 42
Mercury 6, 26, 31
Messier, Charles 6
moons 4–5, 8, 24, 26–27, 30, 32–33, 40, 42
Newton, Sir Isaac 17
Oort Cloud 12
Orion 38
rockets 4, 24, 30–32, 36–38
Roman, Nancy 9
satellites 18–19, 24, 34
Saturn 27, 32
Shepard, Alan 31
sky 4, 6, 8, 15, 17, 22, 42
solar system 4, 9, 12, 24, 26–27, 42
Soyuz 30, 34
spacecraft 24, 26–32, 34, 38–40
Space Shuttle 28–29, 36–37
Stardust 13
stars 4, 6–8, 10, 14–15, 18, 22, 24
sun 4, 6, 8–9, 11–12, 14, 20, 27, 29
supernovas 18
telescopes 4, 12, 16–20, 22
Tereshkova, Valentina 28
universe 4, 6, 9, 20
Venus 6, 26
Vostok 28, 30
Voyager probes 27